Divine Honors

WESLEYAN POETRY

Books by Hilda Raz

What Is Good
The Bone Dish

HILDA RAZ

Divine
Honors

Wesleyan University Press

Published by University Press of New England
Hanover and London

Wesleyan University Press
Published by University Press of New England, Hanover, NH 03755
© *1997 by Hilda Raz*
All rights reserved
Printed in the United States of America
5 4 3 2 1
CIP *data appear at the end of the book*

May I see what I have tried not to see.

——CYNTHIA MACDONALD

. . . divine honours will be paid to shallow depressions in the ground, domestic pets, ruined windmills, or malignant tumours.

——W. H. AUDEN

Contents

Prologue

I

II

III

IV

V

Epilogue

Prologue

Repair

In my house, men tear out the floor:
hammering, then wood splits—
hour on hour. You almost need
safety glasses for this work, the blond says
and truly, as I go for the phone,
the kitchen is now rubble. Delight
a paste bubble in my throat. If anger is tangible
here it is, a danger to these men
who let fly plaster, the smell of something old
letting go. They unmake what I made
with my life, or where I made it.

Narrative Without People

The soaked books lip open in piles.
The shelves stoop, slough paint.
The doors, their locks sprung, hinge air
open to weather, gulp rain.
Something here enters the trees.

If we believe in ghosts, white pearl
shadows the batten and boards. Rust
runs on the shelves. The sounds on air
wail, a nail in the thumb. Stickers
underfoot poke holes.

In rafters, wings or the suggestion of wings
rend air, whoosh of rubbish, burnt rubber
hooks for skeleton elbows. Ash,
dry sift through moist fingers
in a room where everything's mold.

Let's consider the consequences

only,
the damage,
the number of bricks cracked
in the passageway, doors swollen
by water-rot, frames to pare down,
mildew to scour, how much
to seal up, or seal out.
                    Let's count, yes, quantify
so we can sort the pile of damp clothing, the
discarded underwear with stains, the breakfast napkins
to hang out, hang on line the number of bodily fluids, mixed,
the shrinking lengths of divisions, weights of bias . . .

Now you have a notebook, pages filled with digits, the sweet
wise voice of the wire turning, connecting, recommending measure,
    a count,
the quantifying of the salt and the sugar,
                    "Well, now
you have the damage report, the bottom line, the sum.
Consider the lilies of the field, how they sway in wind
without reference to your pages, how little they care
for laughter or the dour voice, the smile tucked under the chin,
the complaint, the whine, how—if nothing else—you have
your dear cornea, lungs that puff and inflate their wings, lucky
muscle of the calf, the knee, if we could cut an oval and put
the celluloid disc in place how we would see movement, the universe
shifting and settling down in its elliptical orbit, add the catch
    in the stars
breath makes."

So you are advised to burn the notebook, its pages,
the maps and wire measure of damage and move on, move along

until what happens is only a measure of forgetting, detaching
distress, your upset, your dyspepsia from the air of the orchard.
Move ahead and not refer, never refer to
anything other than the sweet taste in your mouth of breath,
the steady blood beat, the road hot and loud under your feet,
    infinite.

Isaac Stern's Performance

Here plants—gold and dry—rustle up
green at soil's edge.
Music roils in the room
where I wait, my chest holding even
at the scar's edge.

Whatever chances I took
paid off and now I have only
the rest of my life to consider.
Once it was a globe, an ocean
to cross, at least a desert—
now a rivulet, or a blowhole.

"I remember it was like a story,"
Rampal said on the radio.
"He told you the Beethoven concerto."
I am telling you cancer.

I am telling you like moisture
at soil's edge after winter, or
the bulb of the amaryllis you brought
raising stem after stem from cork dirt,
one hybrid flower after another unfurling
for hours, each copper petal opening its throat so
slowly, each shudder of tone—mahogany, coral, blood—
an ache, orgasm, agony, life.

Part I

I Hear the Name of the Moon and Am Afraid

Squeals, groans, chirps and whistles like red birds
pinched in the crotches of yews
and their pollen song, beaks.

Or window on rain, fire
thorn tossed down by the instrument of his hand
aloft, thumb letting go of the nape,
apex a great height, noise like a body breaking
on ground.

Hiss, splatter pattern of wave,
wire at the nadir holding the blood fan closed,
blood fan open as red as a cardinal, an orange,
the moon with her blushing face, liquid earphone
static through hot bindings where I toss and listen
to the breakup, earth forcing flesh into new shapes
whir and chitter of arm raising, arm falling, this arm, her name.

Weathering / boundaries / what is good

Your sweet silence, your hands, skin, your mouth.
On the telephone, sleepy, the son of my body.
The sun on my body. His alarm clock ringing. His birthday.
She, matter-of-fact, cool, saying what she knows, promising
to discover what she doesn't know, at the library. Daughter
of my body, Persephone and I Demeter. You with your $125 worth
of spring bulbs divided three ways, three friends, three graces.
We plant them together, warm earth in the garden where your
mother watches, who has cancer too. I make stew—you bring
veggies I cook with meat—and rice custard. You build onto our
patio garden. The patio is rich and crunchy with acorns. Cat and I
stand on the driveway—warm—to find Orion. Now
you are naked and sleeping as I write. Dear God, keep us all safe. My
breast is healing well. I am supple of body. My spirit what? Still at
home in my body.

Cancer is one of the few internal diseases that can be cured. I am a
person who has cancer
now.

You show me fronds of prairie grasses, beige/lavender in sun in
your garden—sun, sun all day—in high 70s—on your garden. On
ours.

Waiting for oncologist with you, v. scared. I'm still me, same me no
matter what he says. Biopsy report shocks me. You say, "So you
know more than the doctor?"— you with me all afternoon, read
report with me. Necrotic tissue. Adjacent cells abnormal. We go
shopping, for a walk. His nurse says, "Recovery is partially depen-
dent . . ." on my attitude. I buy an expensive purse in the shape of a
pouch, what's missing in my body, that last year's thievery. She

speaks about her dream of ribbons and banners, floating upward into light, and her ecstatic sense of losing individual boundaries, losing them and merging into the natural universe. I am fascinated and afraid.

To Explain

The future is what does not happen—Colette

The euphorbia shot a pale rilled tube
toward the light, so all week
I have been grieving, pouring deep gutturals
into the stone edgings of the back garden,
down on my knees, seeming to dig the impatiens.

Nobody heard me but the shade and rain in air.
I must have seemed from a distance
doubled over a dumbbell (what you call weights)
so deeply did I hold my knees to rock
minutes at a time, then stop.

Then once on Sunday as the sky cleared for an hour
I wondered how to say
why I couldn't say
words had gone
in their ashy fans,
and only the wrap of my body
around loss, stayed.

Mu

. . . the old root giving rise to mystery was mu, *with cognates* MYSTICAL *and* MUTE. MYSTERY *came from the Greek* muein *with the meaning of closing the lips, closing the eyes.*

—Lewis Thomas

Misery a block in the head
a block I hum mmmm through, the way mother
mmmm helps me move to. Umber attaches to shadows
in hedge-ribbons. Feet mmmmmmmm, hit-sounds like murder
stitched to lips, the miles, hummm, eyes shut shuttered, cement walk
studded with dark I'm afraid mmmmmo
and now I am come alone at midnight onto the pineneedles of the
    park.

I am come to say good-bye in the dark but my mouth won't open.
What opens is my eye to the open edge of the metal tunnel under
the curve of the spiral slide I'm afraid to rise to. I'm standing at the
base to cry out at midnight Whose children will come down? Who
bashes into my arms so we open our mou ths to this cadence no no
no no mmm mommy up again to ride the big slide they and I falling
into the dark air. Open is the mouth of the metal tunnel.
Tomorrow, mmmmu, the knife.

Coming Down with Something

Black plaques, the windows
give back my face framed
by its noose of hair
and snow, one on one side
the glass, the other out
in the cold with bushes.

Sleep shoved away
by prickers of pain
flickers with streetlights
now off now on
as the cold limbs shiver.

What's gaunt and thin
deep in the body thickens
with phlegm—someone's
hungry some woman
with child and flies touching
at breast and forehead.

I take tea from my kitchen,
a clear mix of water and leaves,
mild, pale, the color of saffron
or urine, like blood like petals

like the robe she wears
over her gray body
impacted with jewels in gauze
smuggled past her husband,
to come here for surgery.

Maybe an aspirin would help.
Certainly something's swollen under our eyelids.

Fish—Belly—Mound

Press in hard to hurt
nine times, twice or more
with your thumb,
the other hand on
that puffed up place.
Thumb rigid and forefinger
a rictus. Tight fist,
fingers merged. Now
peace will flood you,
an overwash from some
ocean of light.

We lay head to toe, neighbors
on tables for treatment, both ill,
both having lost too much to mention.

The side of my body, numb forever,
my clothes hid, still drifted on.
He smiled through a red beard
as our attendants strapped on electrodes.
And the while his naked foot jerked
and kicked and we talked, I pressed
and pressed and now have come home
to shadows where I flail and sink
in light these words swim through,
my fingers a net he tried to weave.

"Two Are Better Than One . . . For If They Fall, the One Will Lift Up His Fellow; But Woe to Him That Is Alone When He Falleth, For He Hath Not Another to Help Him Up."

. . . opened my chest
. . . opened my belly.
You stayed close
your food bowl empty
your feet unclean. The steppes in your head
filled with wind, static, a glow of sand and grit.
Or were you only sleeping those days
you sat by my bed, our hands touching,
the concave round of your skull
a focus mirror, your eyes radiant?

Several times when I slept
you lifted the phone and whispered:
Later, sick, I knew whom you spoke to.
God! Your handmaiden, her fruit cheek
rosy with health, not bloat.
The camellia she brought me
floated in round water its petals
germane—the only flower in that
floral room I could see, night or day,
follow with my bare shoulders, shiny,
intact above the bandage wrapped like skin
in moonlight, in midnight shadow.

In the mornings, in window sun I dozed
and woke repeatedly, myself camellia
on the skin of the hospital bed.
You never left me.
Now I call you scar.

Getting Well

If I get well . . . I can take a walk in the snow and eat a red apple.— Anne Truitt, *Turn*

You gave me four fair hairs
from your head, locked in the pages
you left Monday morning in my mailbox,
a sign of the passion of your reading.

You would have me know how to write
an essay, commissioned, on the stuff of my life
on this model, Truitt's, or any other
we might find together, the pleasure

of our reading in concert as colleagues
hiding our camaraderie in health,
your sure recovery from the disease
I'm sure will take me off.

So I touch the binding, unsure
of what you mean to say. Work
can keep us alive to the world?
Writing down some truth will help?

What I know today has something
to do with your hair, caught
in a book's pages. Fair
you stand up in the world

to walk. Fair, you sit down
in the sun to read, your head
bent down to eat an apple. Here,
you draw in the breath of the air
and breathe it out so we can write.

For Barbara, Who Brings a Green Stone in the Shape of a Triangle

From ocean
this porous shape
indisputably green
color I tell you
of healing, the color
I have chosen around me
like a vapor, this towel
on my shoulders, its green
drape an air over my scar,
then a shirt I pull over my head
and let fall for the green
lint-shed filaments of healing, moss
some ancestor might bind up with spit
and press onto my breast, no, the space
where my breast has been.
                         Yesterday
for the space of an hour, a woman
came here with her child, raised
up shirt, her breast was flesh.
The child pulled where her nipple
is, and touched his mouth
to her and filled himself.
She talked as he drank.
I listened to nipple,
a hiss of milk.
Miracle.

In your photos of green ocean
and boats, a line of women in green air,
their arms muscular, pulls against green water.
Their breasts are bare.
One, yours, shows a faint scar

my skin wears.
                              In the past year
I have given up four of the five organs
the body holds to call itself woman.
                              Green
healer, today my body carries
in its clever hand the triangle
sea gave up to you
and you gave me.

                    I press it to my chest,
empty of nipple, of milk, of nurture,
and feel you there: friend, lover
of women, teacher. You speak to me
each green vowel of the life language.

Day-Old Bargain

Bargain tarts, raspberry, goose,
he said, don't write about that
surgery, women who have hacked off write
all parts and natures of women
who lose food in the bottom parts
of refrigerators, onions, scallions,
sour tomatoes, tiny cocktail weenies
lost in the airless dark write
When you give over your breast
to cancer, for God's sake don't
write about it.

Write about silliness, holding hands
in sandboxes, small girls playing fudge-
and-find-me-alley-tag at dusk, Rochester,
state of pubescent, New Yorka roonie.

. . . day I learned to drive aimed car
at horizon and floored it. Got there.
God in color, no cable, firsthand.
Going and coming back I thought I'd live.

Not much for visions, still at sink soaking
pinkies in sweetalmond suds, I heard Mom.
Come on home, she said. Scared the witless bejeebies
out of me. Next day I opted for surgery.
Cut that mama off and saved my life.
Big daddy surgeon said right on the mark, sweet honey.
It was done.

He's got a girlfriend works at his office, don't you know,
she thinks he's licorice stick swinger. I caught them

hugging in the mimeo room. Ain't nothing to it, he said,
rolling his cup of a palm over the scar. Mmmmmm-mmmmm,
this hillock is a sweet raisin, roll over baby, pour me out.
Okeydokey.

What came next in the woods, woolly dark trees
don't give a fudge if what's hugging them hard
dents in two places. I hang on for dear life.
Filled pockets with seedpods, got bulbs
I shoehorned into clay pots for life's sake.
Nevertheless the disc shone hard, or didn't.

Breast/fever

My new breast is two months old,
gel used in bicycle saddles
for riders on long-distance runs,
stays cold under my skin
when the old breast is warm;
catalogue price, $276. My serial number,
#B-1754, means some sisters under the skin.
My new breast
my new breast is sterile,
will never have cancer.

Once every sixty years
according to the Chinese calendar
comes the year of the golden horse.
Over me your skin is warm,
sweetgel, ribbontongue, goldhorse.
You suck the blank to goosebumps.

HowmIgonnaget there when you're gone
back to your youngthing, sweetcurl?
He moans over your back
twitching your buttons raw. My scar
means nothing to him, a mapletwirl
a whirligig, your center and maypole.

Death waits in the book, the woods,
the TV, the helicopter blades merging
over the house, your hair a fine curl
mist over your haunches, smooth hook near.
You'll curl red over him when I'm under
the ash, gone, all mind or nothing.
Who the hell loves a tree?

Don't tell me on the phone your voice
a fine ringing replica of mine that you've
got sickies, fever, ticks from the job
you won't worry about don't I either
you nut, you bitch dog mother I bred you
out of leaves and mash my blood on the floor
my liver colored placenta curled in a cold bowl.
Who do you think you are with my sick breasts
on your chest. Oh God let me live to touch her
working out the next generation of women.

Part II

An art that heals and protects its subject is a geography of scars.
—Wendell Berry

Sarah's Response

Research is what she promises to do for me,
right now, immediately, she knows whom to call,
where to go, or she'll find out, I'm not to worry,
what there is to know we'll know. And soon?
I beg, far worse than any child terrified
of disappearing, held down only by the thread,
her voice, pulled through the wire at 20,000 megawinds.

She calls when she finds out the bad news and the good
to promise a package: tradition mandates gifts
to make it better. A kiss is what I want, her hand
in mine. But this is what she sends: a box.

The huge carton is heavy, cardboard walls they
let me batter until I get to what's inside
intact within a web of tape and swaying,
entire six foot stalk of brusselsprout,
a hundred knobs or more, each perfect head,
enfolded pattern. I know her message instantly.

In the world that gave us life, or takes it from me,
beauty so precise and orderly if seen by microscope,
or cell biopsy, or tissue through the light
is what divided cell from cell and made her mine,
and him and her, and you, dear reader, whose gel-filled eye
reads out this message written two years later by my pulsing hand
to honor her, my harmonious daughter far away
whose play is radiance. Let her live.

Sarah Among Animals

— Priam's Green Birdwing

Night. The elephant in his pen
waits patiently for Sarah.
His vast ears inflate like sails
as his head, the size of a ship,
veers toward her compound.
His great foot lifts.

Among her butterflies,
a golden handkerchief bordered
with jet draped on her fist,
Sarah listens. She wants to go.
In her veins the thin blood flows.
Were she able to enter the field of light
her arms would flood with veins, and lift.
She lifts her shoulders, shrugs off his charge.
Night. The arc sails on.

Sarah's Head / 16 March, Four Months after Surgery

First the jaw goes, teeth and all
hinges, intricate slivers of bone.
Then silence. Then the brain pan
opens its lid, falls over
with the velocity of a hard-pitch
baseball, spit everywhere. Then nose
in comic relief pops off, a sound
like old bubblegum. What's left?
Light on trees, on sidewalks. Magnolia.

Into the null that clay head cries,
huge skull forced back against
scream's lift, pulled from the void
by Sarah's hands. It rests between glass shelves
on a bronze collar, jagged edges cut to hide
the scar from neck wrenched
out of gray earth: no torso, only sob
out of the gape of this head's loud mouth, and mine.

I conjure comfort with a table set with pottery bowls,
each open like my cupped hands for her newborn head,
tomatoes resting there,
chives the color of amaryllis skin before the bud
breaks open, round bread,
and soup from cabbage and potatoes,
most homely food to nourish me
and a friend, mother of daughters both.
A spring feast. All I can do.

Sarah Fledging

Soft feather heart
blue jay and thrasher
and eagle's down she has gathered,
each nail smoothing each barbed shaft
oiled so her fingers shine.

Meadowlark and finch, cardinal,
the junco, right-upside-up nuthatch,
feather skim on teak where she dips
from a bowl to chamois
against afternoon chill,
pulls her needle through
blood spots dried mahogany.

Flutter heart of feather bowl
as she shakes loose another
amber and dove wet pebble
from the patch by her elbow,
reaches, gathers each shaft for a linen loop,
and waxes and ties off.

Whirl, circle, and wave of feather
jackdaw, hawk, the golden swift
scooping mosquitoes from the backyard lathehouse,
her hands reach to steady the softening cloak—it quivers,
air from the floor vent—she turns.
And now she reaches for the lamp and rises.

Sarah's Waltz

—for Randall Snyder

Now she is gone she is dancing, here
in the kitchen, the oven cold,
bare table a platform
as she pounds her feet—one two three—
soles rosy with henna,
the old teak's oils rising to meet her
to warm her as she twirls, linseed floating her
as she bows, and dips, and bends to us,
and now she raises her arms.

Years ago I grew her
as easily
as the clay pot holds
the primrose.

In her hands as she turns, light
catches and flashes
on crystalline bells
she has fashioned,
carries and tosses,
and catches and releases
into this silence their chime.

Wherever you are, Composer,
hidden behind the arras,
woven into the wheat hanging,
icy drop swaying on its filament
fracturing the moon
as she pivots and whirls

and scatters her clamor,
please capture for us Sarah's heartbeat.
Sound it now.

Balance

Circular ear ornament inlaid with a mosaic of turquoise, mother-of-pearl, lapis lazuli, red Spondylus shell, and green stone, surrounded by a shell ring and border of gold beads.
        —Chimu culture, northern coast of Peru

Postcard from your drawer, daughter,
when the need comes and I
pull on the handle to open, take,
and send away some message: come!

The last gift of earrings I gave
came from India, silver lace fobs
hung from a scrolled wire, tiny malachite tongues
at the tips: Happy Birthday!

The last gift of earrings I got
came from Indonesia, silver half globes
with a golden nipple on each domed center, ear breasts
we joked, touching and touching: Live!

The lobes of my ears are fleshy and large, flushed
with health and sturdy for ornament. To pierce each
I employed the services of a surgeon, bribed
my best friend with a martini to come along.
In the waiting room she held my hand.
On the surgical table I stayed still while the nurse
measured and marked with charcoal the equidistant point
on each lobe where the needle would go in.

Tattoo the blank breast with a nipple,
alternative advice but I hold out
for an ornament. In the long silver winter

I recovered from surgery I pinned each day
to my shirt some concoction of old buttons
from her grandmother's legacy. She glued together
what I seemed to need, pin for nipple I wore, day in day out.

Now I fancy some commissioned shape of lapis lazuli
Yeats might like, or I fancy exactly in the proper shape
of a woman who nursed babies two years of her lengthening life:
some mother-of-pearl drops for milk, some blue veined marble
for the hardness of full breasts, some silky pin back, something new
and fabricated by hands, by my daughter's human hands.

Order

This time, Sarah fabricates a pin
I'll wear each day on my pocket.
Over the phone when I say why
she laughs and laughs, my far daughter
with her "humongous breasts from Hell,"
at this folly, that I in my sadness
choose to have two ornaments,
one flesh, and one she'll cut.

Two months later she comes home
to fix a tiny silver moon
with dark brass nipple on my chest.
She pins it fast to heal my loss:
a breast she made, as I made her.

Axe-earrings, abalone shell

in leaf-humus by the river, buried
at the base of the arc, a light she watched
fall, sun-fall on silver fastenings, thrown
from her earlobes, flesh
scarred, healed, for the holding
of ornaments. What I wanted. A gift.

Leaf humus smell around her, rising
like water, red from sun, red falling
from body, scarred, sealed,
healed, an ornament now.

Path over bridge, scar over mound
healing now, puckering, leaf mold
over earrings, gift snatched from lobe,
thrown, thrown an arc, light
flaring from silver hooks, thrown
away into river humus, leaf rot.

At my elbow, holding, a woman.
At my breast, that news, skin
smell of the new born, borne out
into this world of melt and fracture,
here at my side, holding, woman.

Birth

Hours taking hours
to pass, no gray
to the sky, no moon,
only a light triangle
blurring to signify
you've taken

What? Nothing.

In this dream the mushroom
picker's light shines
on a white swelling.
Everywhere is pale
or pure
darkness. She is
picking me
she is picking me out.

I choose you.
I am not blindfolded
or surprised. Palms
touching palms are buffed
pale in the mushroom light
before dawn.

Here we are rocking,
each forehead a fulcrum,
my arms crowning your head
a great weight holding us
down. Now we are crosslegged
in the scorching light.

The touching of your ribs against my thighs
has nothing to do with me.
I tell everyone here this truth.

Part III

Was there not a way of naming things that would not invent names, but mean names without naming them?—Gertrude Stein

Opening / Working / Walking

If you were to go to one of these factories . . . you'd see dozens of girls standing there pushing levers. That's how difficult it is.——William Dorward, *The New Yorker*

That's how difficult it was,
snow geese dropping into their images.
And the earth, still opened, steaming,
a gash where she disappeared.
What could I do but stare down
and wail? My tatters at wrist
and throat flapped and the crackle
of wheat under my feet was all I heard
for weeks. No wonder then I returned to the factory.

I am her mother!
In this city I sing——the enemy is everywhere——
walk in a ring each noon, rifle cradled under my shawls.
The others? I tell you we are mourning. They say nothing.
What they're making is silence of these off hours,
sun hot and familiar smoothing our dark veils.
Some days the dust of earth punctures,
surrenders its mud with teeth, a thigh-bone.

Now the body remembers its openings
without banners, the slogans we chant mornings
to the clank of levers, a din we carry home.
Coals, then out into market again.
We circle the pavement trailing our cloths
of silence, our lace a small singing——the enemy is everywhere.
What crowded place have we come to, women, to be grieving and
    armed?

Hey You

You don't have to be a farmer to love soybeans.
You don't have to be a rocket scientist to talk
on the radio. Beginning Thursday, anyone
can address mayhem in far places, assassins
with animal names, gangs of them hurting us.

Trouble is, life isn't worth more than breath
in a troubled chest, the rattle, the rictus
without cloud, a check mark of dark against sunset
but not quite night. Darling, where your freckles
meet your empty eye sockets, sparklets erupt.
Nothing language about it.

You should have heard that knock-down chicklet
rock out her grief. Honey, no mom can soothe
her sore throat: ululation and a life so wracked
a bamboo thicket looks like a Serta Sleeper.

                              God!
Whatever mountain you've taken up,
come read us a story. We need to sleep
when our paint brushes wear down to nubs,
our reds and yellows evaporate on the pale margins
or drip past the wash.

                    We burst from your forehead
obediently primed, pumped up to meet.
Merging is what we do best after all, our boundaries
so blurred what's her worry is our worry: a good job
is what we've done, heads rolling off our shoulders
into the mass grave, our torsos blurring as they tumble.

Hey, you there. You listening?

Grieving, she hits the red fox

—for Vera Spohr Cohen

crossways. In fog. High beams
backed up. His head turned to her.
She knows his eyes flare.
He is gone under her wheels.
She could turn.

He is gone from her long before, ash,
to the floor of earth just buried,
body heavy with shadows.

The car speeds in its tunnel of light.
She could turn.
                Spirit lover!

Not even the black mirror
draws your eyes from the gravel.

Mapping / Bleating

I think chemistry has much to gain from reviving the personal, the emotional, the stylistic core of the struggle to discover and create the molecular world.
　　　　　　　　—Roald Hoffmann, "Under the Surface of the Chemical Article"

The graphic depiction of molecules . . . Hoffmann argues, is so central to the science of chemistry that its conventions and ambiguities deserve reflection. A chemist faces the same difficulty as a landscape painter: how to represent three-dimensional shapes in two dimensions.
　　　　　　　　—Emily Grosholz, "Roald Hoffmann's Praise of Synthetic Beauty"

My fingers, mine, my fingers
instructed as ice molecules
in trees, now on this airplane wing out the window,
to address the subject of
no, not war (planes and missiles
we pop as objects on the nightly news,
the morning news we set our short wave
scanner to)
but death, a subject
breathing
used to seem to catch up to
and expand as atoms of air, pure ether.

My fingers move at random, push
the words out on this paper. Fog
smothers the wing tip. I can't see lights.
Am dizzy.

Where are we going? You are moving radon
gas over the sensor box. He buckles the web.
She tucks the head of a newborn (thumbs
a half moon around each apricot ear) under her rib. I am

aloft, yes, tucked in. I am going to smell,
no, say right, apprehend death, its
molecules in cells cut out,
excised; only a prim removal
of some feeder flesh, her breast. Mine's
gone so I'm immune. My friend gives me this gift
of witness. Once there, I'll hold her daughter's ear. Going,
my chest is laved in apricot lotion under the linen of my shift.

What next? A band of clay braided at the lip
of the gift cup wrapped in my underwear,
milk spotted with chocolate floaters, or brandy
in steam, tea steeped until mash of pattern
predicts the final outcome: death. When we land on earth
first thing is, I'll unpack this stoneware cup, brew comfort.
Still, to be honest, down small or up here,
the light plaids, curtains golden on cotton, and I'm bleating.

Trope

Edith Wharton "did her best writing in her fifties and sixties . . . Her appetite for life seemed to grow and sharpen as her time ran out . . . she described herself as 'an incorrigible life-lover and life-won-derer and adventurer.'"——Vogue

She hates us, our race, our hair,
each day we breathe in air.
She loves the pits under our feet
and listens to my arias on each escape,
her green eyes avid, her rough laugh
pulled up from her navel. The closer I draw failure
on our paper table mats,
the faster she erases. At the moment
of catastrophe—the lumps, the rejection form,
the denied promotion, the deaths of sons—

she is at the door, her arms open,
her leather bag filled with books
and perfumes, fresh flowers. Endlessly
over bad dinners, she outlines and synthesizes
strategies, asks questions, listens to amours,
then divides the check scrupulously, right down the middle.

She keeps us close, who are not her equals,
for comfort, in case she's wronged, or sick,
and her greed for what we have
is filled with radiance and a miraculous energy.

Our triumphs she dismisses out loud as politics
— she is right, undoubtedly—but our hurts
are the real thing. She knows the tone
of the true howl, the keening, the bruise

at the throat, the last gasp, and she wants to be there
when the ambulance wails, the police beat down the door
and someone gives up all that oxygen.

Where I write, *J'accuse*, she adds illuminations.
She clips articles with your name in them.
And though she is brilliant and speaks well, she holds scatter
and babble close, a friendly shield. When your breast is taken
she divides her bulbs and brings you half, pushes onto her knees
and drags you down. At the oncologist's office, there she is
reading over your shoulder. On the day you die, you know
she'll go for your eyes while digging in her bag for coins for Charon.

Sow Sister

The sow sister in barnyard mud
shifts her crinolines
to one side and lifts her thigh.
Sun beats on her knuckle bones,
"Sow-sister, sow-sister, mind me."

Not that she doesn't hear
but staggers to the far grass
staggers and sleeps, her hair
drying fast, stiffening.

Sow-sister, psst, wake up!
Past patience I am boiling you
to nonsense, your hocks and breasts
bone-bold. Your oils melting.
You must thrive, burlap sadness folded
into packet-statues, your cousin beaver's pelt
stiffened with glue mercury into hats, shining.

Ah, no? Well, so I will tell you a story.
Lie down in my wild mud, slippery and warm.
Now you will hear whuffling far off in a bottle
and the heavens will open with malt. Cooked,
in your mouth you'll come to know sift
of slivered almonds in vanilla sugar, this story.

Bernini's Ribbon

—an aerial sculpture by S. Roth-Kent

Someone else's voice in this lobby,
clear but unfamiliar, "I was an executive secretary
before I went to med school,"
and again a familiar male voice saying,
"You don't *get* it, do you?"—the female tag
at the end of the sentence, "do you?"—
as in *The Exorcist* when a small girl opens
her mouth and out comes the voice
of the devil like musk, a shock.
Getting personal with someone new,
unfamily, unknown, someone to help, to help
you.
    So in the course of the day's spiral
from garble comes story: she was healing
at last, the edges of crust dissolving in warm
water, surface only one foreground of many
textures, only one shiny surface leading the eye
out and away until color takes over the job,
lifts with purples and golds and sulphur, galls
the eye up to the proscenium arch, the ceiling
higher beyond, and Bernini's Ribbon
through high air a dropped clue
to follow: voices, the maze.

Petting the Scar

—for Alicia Ostriker

You know what? I don't want a brave death,
faithful children mopping up after my body,
sweet thing, nubbly fissures and skin so soft
it's silklike. Let my daughter wail at the side
of her lover's bed, her heart in its tough covering
beating powdery as a butterfly's wing.
My son, oh no, let him turn up his torso
to the Greek sun, his heartscar sexy, raised
on his dark skin.

So what are we to do tonight, finished with passion,
roaming our rooms, our thumbs hooked
under the spines of books, notebooks by each chair,
forbidden smokes flushed and fats scoured away?
You tell me to reach under my shirt and pet the scar.

Did you hear about the lozenge of blood on the binding
of our friend's new book, who is trying hard in a far country?
I forgot to tell you. "If I can bear to touch it," she said.
"Yet," surely you'd add.

Under my robe—I must put down my pen to do it—
my palm finds chill: this is not a metaphor
but an image, true, a fact: I swear it.
No pouty lip the color of eyelids. A cold blank.

But the scar!
Riverroad, meandering root, stretched coil, wire chord, embroidery
in its hoop, mine, my body.

Oh, love!

Teaching, Hurt

Bradshaw, Nebraska, near York, forty-eight miles
the spring of the heart
loud under its breast
wild heart at its single lesson,
spring of sterile apples, trees a pyramid of white
spectacle overflowing buttermilk at twilight,
spring of buttermilk, the body's affairs,
heart broken under its absent breast the beat so loud
she fancies they can hear it thud
in a room loud with her perfume's diversion.

Spring teaching again, gone to the highway by six,
alone, fields ripening in some color
she can't name. Bradshaw, Bradshaw,
rhymes with bedsore, rhymes with bad law,
lockjaw, she can't find a place
to work without disturbing someone.
At lunch the teacher names her boys
twins, and an older. "It could be worse," she laughs
out loud, delighted, and someone whispers yes,
the first child has cancer in his brain.

Into this mess, new life:
week-old Peking ducks, and mallards, gray brown
and plain, some with green heads
you can't tell yet which is which, girl from boy;
a Hamburg chick, sole survivor of the trip from Omaha,
flat comb, wide tail feathers, an exotic;
and Partridge Cochin, feathers down to their golden feet,
colored like pheasants; twelve babies in a Wheat Chex box
small as first graders who make the circle work
holding chicks onto their newspapers. The water dish

overflows onto the floor of the lunchroom where the kids
make nests of their legs to sit watching
and she hunches over them, hungry to see
what they see, to see them.

Riddle

I'm the one who pumps all day
all night to let you live.
All I get in return is broken.

This one from Scott, grade nine,
on the day the kids say
they like me, write hard
as I roam their aisles in Crete
the spring after the year
I had cancer, two years after
my body emptied.

This from life, the body blow
the medicine ball lets swing
from the rafters in the gym
and you in the way, the thump
and thud as your blood rushes
to cover up, the kids in attendance
as the bruise begins to color.

Outside hail pummeling the car,
my minotaur thudding
against ribs bruised but holding,
the flesh cage, against his rampages.
And I drive like hell in the din.

Today I am eating again. Donuts in the lounge
soothe my throat, enter my empty belly.
Coffee. A plaque in italic on oak
a creed about acceptance. I'm trying.
In my ninth grade year, the elastic band
in my underpants stretched out—all seven pair,

each day of the week an accident. I was thin.
Who could love me again in a world so dangerous I was food?

Now, each breath a gift, the soar in air
of hawks on the highway searching for road kill:
some sure sign I'm present. This world is dangerous.
I hurt in the teachers' lounge where TV dribbles
and the choral teacher warbles his vibrato
in answer to the second grade aide, a soprano.
Their voices braid in time to cover my hiccup.

Part IV

A fetish is a story masquerading as an object.
— Robert J. Stolles, M.D.

Chigger Socks

She told how
on her wedding eve
playing badminton at dusk
with friends on the lawn,
she in shorts and high socks,
her last chance, she thought,
to be a girl, though she was thirty
and carried divorce decrees
among her important papers;
so she leapt into air after feathers
and grew shiny and damp at forehead and heel
and threw herself, finally, into alfalfa grass
by the net to rest at the horizon,
and drink wine, and wrestle with the dogs.

When her mother knocked next morning
and entered the dark room,
she was sitting on tile, feet cold
and aflame with bites, swollen to the knee
twice what you'd think skin can hold of flesh.
By noon, after basins of ice, elastic bindings,
she could stand in her mother's arms and was wed,
lace stretch stockings hiding almost all.

Waking this morning to light breathing
I remember the queen and her iron shoes
dancing her fiery feet off. You're gone.
You entered another shoe to tend another
child or two, forgetting ours, who grew head
to heel under my leather tongue and grew up
and went off. One wears your face exactly,
and I have grown old, my feet pins-and-needles now, cold.

Daylight Savings: Sandy Creek, Nebraska

Between shelves where I work in the dark
the librarian comes to visit. I'm a farmer,
he says, bankrupt. Like many others,
I say, polite, the visiting teacher. He turns pages
of the new book he has come to show me
with a hand minus a thumb.

One book about travel he likes especially.
The cover shows a high-wheeler parked by a fence.
I ride them, he says proudly.
Another book about Nazi resistance in France
shows a child with a spade. Farming, he says.

I don't know how to do this job yet, he whispers,
wondering about his book choices. What do I think?
I think he's doing fine. Books about women,
books about history, books about politics.
Nicaragua with a picture of trees on the front.

On Tuesday nights after school he's learning
EMT, Emergency Medical Training. They don't have doctors
out here. No better way to give time. He's got kids too,
he says, locking up the room for lunch. In the hall
he opens a folder with pictures: broken chests, sutures,
flailed lungs. Over spaghetti I ask if he's ever afraid.
Never, he says. I castrated bulls, dehorned them,
the blood flying, vaccinated for black leg. Some get the vet
for that but I didn't. I never did. I've seen it all.

In the afternoon I teach freshmen and juniors.
One, handsome with a neck hickey, surly and quiet,
writes well about death. In the state hospital for a month
last year, says the teacher. What can I do for him?

Outside spring raises the smell of urine from the fields.
I walk through, breathing what cures.
I watch the sun go down late. Next day at eight-thirty class break
the librarian calls out, "Sure hard to get up these dark mornings."
"Sure is," I say.

Cobb's Hill Pond

The snow at the edge
froze it was so cold
the January he was eleven,
big brother in hockey skates.
Bent over my double runners
his knuckles whitened
at the buckles of my ankle bindings.
Our steam of breath
touched the scarred bench
where I sat, indifferent,
as if the warmth of his body
could never cool down
no matter how thick the ice grew.

I'm seven-and-a-half Sunday.
Papa puts my peach snowsuit
over my head, zips up.
We're going fishing. Big freeze
makes magnolia blossoms mush
but sky's clear. I tote fly
fishing rods for Papa.
We'll go where target rings in the water
are primary colors to break the pond.
Must be the red one calls him in.

You wouldn't say why
you were humming;
you cast
feathers onto water.
Something shiny must've waited
under the pond's surface.
You hitched up your boots,

stumbled off the bank
humming
deeper and farther
until your hips in their rubber trousers
soaked cold—you were shivering.
Then you fell over,
log with only half a side showing,
and lay still.
I ran—stone without slingshot—
around and around
the flower tree
on the bank
until some snap went off
and I flew home for help:
too late, too late:
messenger, bad pebble.

I never saw them again.

Fuss

Vowels, the O of his voice
shaking comics loose from the Sunday paper
his hands on their crinkling
and later the gun in its opened sack
shaken loose, lifted
to the O of his mouth.

We walked through grass to the reservoir
high circle we moved to enter
a girl in patent leather shoes
a man in boots, that stiff uniform
swishing khaki twill.

His voice on the telephone, lift
and catalogue   the possibilities.
What he bought   What he gave to the poor
His resignations
He lay on the metal floor of some car
rich with his blood   rich with his swill
and the round wind fussed for me
Sister   it whispered.

He turned to the door
chalk   his bones whitened
and began to dry
He put the gun
into his mouth and shattered
so he and his bones left me
for good, for ash.

He turned his face to the wall   to plaster of wall
to amalgam of fire and earth   to clay. And he
and his voice left me for air,
for naught the O of his mouth.

Zen: the one I love most holds my tongue

done nothing to deserve this
am something to deserve this
sleep.
　　　If he is right, the world
is a broad river of emptiness,
currents of everything tangible braided
until the banks expand: dark sea
shining within, dark shine flowing.

If he is wrong, each leaf is a needle
of light my skin encloses. Folds over,
petal by petal, until the coal ignites.
Sleep. Emptiness. How to reach shore?

If he is right, I *am* the shore, skin
no barrier to sea, skin sea
the salt molecules twirling,
pain a current, electric swirl in a boiling
we hold. Whether we ask it or not
we are all carried off.

The one I love most carries my tongue in a pot.
Without me it says nothing to our common silence.
Is sea. Hisses out.

Camarada

Oh you with the broken back,
you curled on the bedspread, the curb,
clenched with the knob
of quilt between your thighs,
you hugging your country song—
nowhere to go and no way to get there—
to your chest, that cave with its nubbins
of bat rocks, your friendship,
your camaraderie, your hollow under the house,
you deer.

Safe away from your skin, the hollows
of your rough cheeks, poked holes,
your silk hair I wrap around me,
a gift, a present for someone else
who loves you too. Presumptuous,
a stiff word your tongue bumps into,
presumptuous to suppose she'd turn to you.

Safe in my white room above the nursery,
above the garden, the smokestacks
belching their bones, safe in my history,
the family you wouldn't give birth to,
the home you never had. How do you get
a chair? you ask me. Dummkopf. The shadow
I am on my walls wants you too.

You open nothing. You clamp your music
onto your ears and wind dies down,
rain in its bowl of cinders, the possum
slitches its body through grass— you don't hear.
You have only the cave of your ear to escape to,

a dark place you light with music, a place
so small I can't find you, a place safe but austere.

I am your keeper, your jailer, your truant,
the villain who keeps you from coming out
to play. Our words are babel to each other,
our touch a magic wrapper. Dear loved one,
give me freedom to come and go as I will.
I'll stay home, the fireplace ashes, my fur shoe.

From Your Mouth to God's Ear

Off the cliff, into air, the mother shout
blackberry-jam thick, stirred down
into a soothing lick on the needle-pricked
thumb, from God's mouth to your ear:
Stay put! The clouds won't, that's for sure:
the rabbit, no voice and frozen on the lawn,
won't for long. And you'll have nothing to say
again, as usual. For sure.
Wasn't that old story about a man spinning
straw into gold a lie? Oh? He did it for a girl.

"We don't deserve what we get, but we get what we deserve."

—Phil Condon

Rain pours
into the heart
of the hosta.

Each one
of fifty blooms
opens a throat to the wet,
can scent a room
each flower smaller
than your fingernail.

In the garden for herbs
basil and parsley, tarragon,
you stoop, take our scissors
to a fair chin,
bring in one blossom
leaking.

G: But it's still not all right with you?
K: But it's still not all right with me.
                              ——AWP *Chronicle*

A blend of peppermint/spearmint
for a sick tummy: tummy mint
a poultice for embroidery on ignorance.
Mine's a muslin bag; yours chamois for vision,
poked with herbs: feverfew, forget-me-not,
sweet nettle, powdered thistle, rue
for dreams: marriage, palm to palm, or
no distinctions, races, genders, each to each:
dear Darwin in his garden, counting earthworms.

They'll feed on us, our knowledge mingled
under a thatch of gravegrass. Dear me,
you stuff your pack as I embroider,
prick my thumb on floss flowers, pure silk,
the one substance eugenics could not touch
in its indifference. My tummy hurts.
No poem can salve me, or beach grass
in sun. I deliver you to hear
a lecture. I trick myself with tea.
We go our separate ways again. We try and try.
Yet what rhymes casts up her barbs.

Mutation Blues

Got blues so harsh they take my breath
Got blues so strong I'm on my head
with your fussing and praising and denying and saying
sweet honeybun you're the mystery of my life.

Each day I wake up praying you're gonna stay.
Each day I raise my nose up to the sunny sky
sighing God above you gave me what I wanted
Sweet God above I begged you for a chance.

My breath comes up goes down my cinnamon throat
breath clangs hard in my head and in my ears.
Sweet honey stick I gave away my heart to
what's natural is what I give to keep you here.

Close to me you watch my eyeballs swell.
Far from me you turn your head away.
I wear a rag and screwturn on my skullcap
but you never notice me at all until I'm gone.

Oh lord above please tell me what to make up out of
Oh lordy above I don't know what I know.
I'm a honeybun that's used her days for nothing
and now I'm going home I don't know where I've been.

Insomnia Again

My friend, who is nearing eighty, calls to praise me,
a recent honor, and says, "Posh" and "Fah" to my worries.
"Conflict," she says,"is the source of life.
Without it we wither."

Is that what keeps us keen? Is that what keeps us up
in the night worrying? We have no stomach
for it. I don't say so but reflect, at 2 AM,
on someone in the Bible, in the fiery furnace,
lean and glistening of muscle. Did he thrash, did he hurl
himself against the hot, locked door? In these versions
of our torments, we do well to remember the finish line:
He got out. The Lord (praised be his name) sent him a friend
with an uzi. Or, the keeper loved him. In their sweat
was lubrication enough he slithered out a hole in the wall.
He was reborn, a ribbon in air.

My other friend has a friend reborn in water,
who walked into the Charles River and drowned.
She was a poet; she wrote of the flood
in the voice of Nemach, Noah's wife,
in the few years of her recent life.
My friend is sad and thinks of leaving teaching.
I'm drinking Ovaltine, myself, in deepening night.
My children's father's mother recommended it
for tension before a truck ground her into earth,
and lactic acid, I've read, is kind to endorphins.
We will be calmed.

Now, so early in the morning custom turns our heads
to the window, we see birds, juncos framed by
clay pots filled with fern and air-climbing hydrangea.

Baskets of tuberous begonias with flushed double cheeks
and single heads. Fuzz of the soft kind, baby leaves.
Fire, water, earth, air: they're what we've got.
The world will rock us. We all go off to bed.

Service

I

Do they hate each other, I wonder,
she who will live on and he who is dying?
I fill their bird feeder with safflower.
Each dip of the orange pitcher scatters seed from its lip
to the earth, in ecstasy. An arc.
A small rain falls down. Bruised light
a nacre over everything.
My breast hurts, shoulder hurts—hurt body—
as I lift my arm to pour, in ecstasy. Alive!
Ready soon to paint their high door.

II

Perhaps I'm ready to paint the high door.
The phone shrills, 4 AM, and I wake
from cicada's trill to cicadas: nothing more.
Far thunder. The rustle the cat makes
reshaping her nest on the floor.
A far train moving cargo.
From the front room, light over the door
where he works all night. Under a microscope once
I watched hooks gouged in paper
by the pen's point, moving,
ink filling in after. A rasp.
And it's morning. Rain.

III

Car/scars

The car with its pocks and scrapes
offends when God knows what's under his trouser band.
Do they mind skin's markings when what's under works on?
I'm having the door painted.

IV

The water fit to drink? he asks.
I put up the canning kettle to boil.
She goes to the grocery for distilled water,
maybe listens to the radio *en route*. Floods.
Thirst, that blessing. I drink and drink from the faucet.
What's under the skin works on in spite of pocks, cut.

V

En route to the barn, their horses hang their heads over thistles,
for sugar. Girth: barrel-bodies, vats hops-colored, caramel, the
safflower bare-skin scars no trouble to hide.
Are their mouths the width of my hips? Breast? Is their water fit to
drink? They mean no harm to the world, you say.
Their muzzles are cut-velvet. Apples.

VI

Fury/night again

Velvet muzzles. They mean no harm
who fit you out. Rain needs the stage now,
chestnuts broadcasting their available stink.
Tuck in your chin, here, sheepskin cup and your tongue cut
on metal, your tongue on sheepskin . . . you'll do no harm
to the world. Thirst. No water, fit or no.

VII

Overheard

Under her skin, poison, but she died well
three years after the doctor said. "I've stopped wondering,"
she said at last, tucking her chin under her tea cup.
No nickering. No sugar, no thistles, no apples, no sass,
a pin through her neck. At the fence everyday,

you'd never have known her, ribs broken from retching.
Once she was fed earth's bounty.
I'm ready now to paint your high door.

VIII

My nightshift covers earth's bounty
erased. A shroud would be worse.
No fit water to drink. Blessed thirst.
He writes all night, drags pen
over paper. Light a nacre over everything.
Night. Thistles. Apples. In my palm
velvet muzzle, water. In my breast, a cut mouth.
In my mouth, tongue's cup. High door freshly painted, my arm
lifting in ecstasy, seed pitcher an arc flung high over rain's
ring on the horizon, broken.

Part V

Hot

That knuckle of bone
under the cat's paw
flies in the sky.

We breathe what sears.
Salt from our faces
cures battered leather.
We drink.

Under the sky's udder
loam fields crack and dry.
We suck tomatoes
grazing the vines
for fluid.

Insects thrive
in laundry bushes
we throw our indigo cloth on
beaten of its smell
to tint the river.
Welts rise.

What's behind the dome of sky
leans down, pushing blue to us
whether we want it or not.
Air inhales cotton's water.

Cracked shoulders
raise our arms like swimmers
to shake lengths of crumpled yardage
over our bodies.
We fall to the fields
that open and close.

Dying

Someone is dying; someone wants to die,
standing by a braid of onions,
purple, dry streamers, string. They pour tea.

Someone's body is crowding,
someone else's is hollow.
Now both bend over teacups.
The window at their shoulders shows
grapes, an arbor, and Look!
a dun cardinal. The red male spies.
All heads rise, bright eyes, the leaves tremble.

Terror: A Riddle

—after Walt Whitman

Like air you seep into my body cavities
and take up residence, open charge accounts,
root, stalk, and flower a perfume of rush
and drum, violet as sunset, a bruise
over stitches. I walk, you walk.
Then I run—if I'm lucky.
Unlucky I lie in the bed or worse,
too weak to rub the ice itch. God!

Want nothing, says her voice so I do.
Then you go away. You're through.

Nuts

to success. The third day lucky
on the job and nothing's changed: I work all day,
I worked all day. Nuts to beauty.
Bikini, music, then the childbed. Inside out
through the door of a birdcage: Margaret Atwood.
Now in the mirror, a sea turtle with goiter.

Nuts to the mirror.
Forty below windchill, she rides her bike
to work, is hit by a truck. Who's freezing
on the radiator is bound to freeze.
Nuts to visitors. They slip on ice like thunder,
clap closed their wimples, rise, then sue.

What's nibbling your liver, kid?
Birdsong. Nuts to praise,
the poet's contract, nuts to quicksilver
in glass, nuts to the fever it measures,
the belly's gripe, nuts to love that only
smells like a vine, to bougainvillea on the tongue,
to ice cream, to blood warm on the palm, nuts
to surgery, the pain it stops, the pain it is.

Lincoln, Nebraska

Here
gray sky and birch trees
an aerie's view
where I work to find
that safe place
safe from silence
from cancer, from isolation,
from the blue flame under the pot
that signals too little oxygen
the breath lost, the skin blue now
and death in Wyuka, underground
border at O street, called Zero
in another place less pristine,
another poem. Meanwhile spring
in the crocus, yellow triangle
at the edge of Love Library as we turn
to enter for the board meeting.

Letter of Transmittal

Herein find one woman, used, in fair shape,
given to excess, too fond of what's personal
to star in meetings, intuitive
rather than learned as we say,
whose favorite pastime is the job
you've offered (which in our service
she defined), whose greatest accomplishment
is drawing breath.

On the office phone we heard
she heard this counsel, part of her job,
to pet the scar, croon to her body,
the surviving parts, sway and cherish
like a lover all that falls easily
into the upturned palm. Representative
of the job she's done.

Her last assignment is her signature, here
at the bottom of this letter. Take her.
We have voted, given voice to her eulogy.
Where she goes now is her own affair.
Our names are below. Take her.
Everything we have been able to do
for her is done. What's left is truly bone.
If you wish it, take her home.

Now

Some problems of self-loathing, worry:
the thumbnail blotched in a bank box
door grows out, three-quarter moon marrow spot
filled out with white bruise travels down
my thumb at regular speed, so when I glance
down it's what I see left of center, not
the odd breast, the malformed scruff
at head, the old thought leaking pain
on the pages from my brain, which ought
to be gainfully occupied with rain
as an emblem of loss and gain, and is not.

Who Does She Think She Is

Risen from the cart,
the sick bed, the steel trolley?
Witch of the world, her roars
hide in waterfalls so small
no human on earth has seen them.

Small, I wander the paths
of the world, dust, a miracle
nose to scoop air, breathing.
Between my skin and spine a thin layer
of cells, a silence.

Who do I think I am,
a solitude, a poor bridge, small beer?
Enough that my eyes focus
on that emerald tree, that spruce,
blue in its huge dying.

Risen again, once more
the heat of my skin
pours radiance, praise,
salt and hops into air, my skin a bracelet
of psalms, my navel invisible, a veil.

Earlier

Life offers up no miracles, unfortunately, and needs assistance.
   —Weldon Kees, "A Distance from the Sea"

Three years since cancer and I seem to live
a smaller person than I was before —
Then: racked by darkness and desire, fear:
whatever needs I could not meet.

For years the baby crying in his crib
and she I bore in blood and ecstasy
seemed hooks to tear me limb from limb
with suffering, theirs far worse than mine,

and at my hands. Who gave them over to my care
must be unfit, a sadist human life can hardly understand
and I, forever loosening skirt or bodice, or my mind,
could only bend to scoop the baby from her bed

or raise my ass or wit to yet comply
with needs I had myself, or didn't, or dimly knew
but learned to satisfy, then damp, and so to die.

Vowels

Holes on the page
the eye picks up,
the ear opens to,
the *I* finds irresistible.

Wide mouth bass
drift on weeds
by the dam's breach.
A lake
in upper New York state,
a pond near Syracuse,
both yield their fish
to the lone fisherman
in autumn, his monofilament line
hissing and dipping over water.
"Watch the bowl the line makes
before fish strike," he calls,
seating bait on his hook.

Or, heather in fields
a purple glazed mist
the bagpiper walks through,
breaking stride
only for the boulder, his pipes
blowing for all Hell to hear.
Get out of there!

He touches her breast with his ear
as she cradles him now, against
an oval to break his heart
so she moans, or he does
touching her here.

He made of the sound a conduit path,
a drumbeat to his heart, a traveling
and when it arrived he exploded and burned,
and fell ashes into the bass of it,
the flower.

So they begot music
and were saved.
And the ewe was in the thicket
well used, and the fish ground
in the mortar, and horseradish
and another year
turned.

Epilogue

Gloxinia / Flicker / Oxalis

Fists toast-rose, the color of your palm
push up through leaves plate sized
no more sturdy than the crockery you broke
throwing out everything soiled. Junk
the dirty pots, the cups with tea . . .

These leaves broken by careless handling
functional enough for buds
thrust out on some time scale
other than ours, furious to be free
of shade, their record of growth
a trajectory very like Louganis
leaving the board, lift, tuck,
his body like a bud
knees tucked into his arms against the fall
held to make a fist
punched through air . . .

Out this window on the copper bowl's lip
where you've made a pool
a bird folds down
not dainty like the chickadee, or the hummingbird
fed with oranges skewered on a bolt
but big enough, hunky like a robin, and bold . . .

The sour wood sorrel, oxalis,
explores the brick
creases the wood mulch
raises umbels like milkweed
flowers rising from the core
in profusion
many colored, like the coat

air wears when soaked with the hose
you hold gently
the spray arc
rising to fall tight in a stream
until you open the nozzle
at the bird bath
and the flicker there
opens her wings in holy light
and the hot body leaps
to mist enfolding all the garden there is
and enters . . .

Recovery

The fingers of the rain are tapping again.
I send out my heart's drum.
Blood stripe on the feathered tulip dissolves into wet.
All night a low thrumming.

Up, up the two-toned hosta
green from sopped earth.
Along your bruised ribs, cream bells.

My Award / The Jews of Lukow

It comes at a good time, I say
across the table next morning
blessed by Muzak floating down
over toast. We talk of children
our life continuing on the planet

where a new study shows the complicity
of tens of thousands of citizens,
good burghers come to watch, staying to slaughter
not coerced as we'd thought
but diligent volunteers—
as Bosnians killing Muslims, Khmer Rouge
the Cambodians, Hutus Tutsies in Rwanda
Turks Armenians through our long human history.

So last night I rose and walked to the stage,
ascended and turned to the lights, to the microphone
as to a lover's mouth, and everyone
standing, clapping . . .

Not mind you that I deserve it
not for anything I put my mind to
only my body's luck until now:
this morning the first rolled leaves
of the straight line of crocus
through arid soil on the driveway strip
at six the sky lighter
better than the deep absence
cold proclaimed all winter
in case I'd forget.

Oh, glad to be here.

And I suppose they in the auditorium last night,
the ones standing, were glad too
so many of us in the ground —
Rose Meile whose mother checked the furnace's clang
while Rose stayed in the kitchen mopping the floor.
Then she was motherless, burned but not up
the explosion a goad to the child
then the woman who helped us all
even with the kind of cancer that took her in.

A walk in the country
myriad of what's wild, that gorgeous catalogue

revived and then the cultivars in our garden
showy, flashy the oranges and florescents
and the natural Stars there with hybrid vigor.

All winter looking up
following the flocks of geese
on their round from Saint Elizabeth's to Home Lake
and back, appearances of the wild:
broad V, exchanged leaders and the muscular flap
in concert. All illusion, the flocks tame
as Romulus and Remus's mom with two human sons to rear.

In recent dreams you say no
to ice cream and won't stay
by the table where my child
is radically changed
nor buy the wire basket
of tomatoes at the farm stand
you speed by like a demon, a ribbon . . .

The man entering

with a cell phone to his ear
takes the next booth.
He has the right to command
our attention from the page.
It's business. Or only a break
from loneliness we all want
deprived of conversation
yearning for the best seller
explaining THE calculus, gorgeous,
or company on the rack.
He orders bacon and a bear claw
pastry held together with butter
such cheap thrills.

Last night at camp
or a conference in a hotel
with crowds
I put forward my best foot
for an encounter with a man so young
he's the rival of my kids,
with a follower younger than he is.
He flirts, I resist
preoccupied as usual with wardrobe.
Next, a cataclysm of nature
some riot, a maniac with a gun.
When I return to the desk
exhausted after hours of eyebeams
you're gone, with her
with my homework, which you lose,
and I'm in the wrong school again.

But look, you two in a corner
over coffee. In my room
the message on the machine

the real thing, you're lost, missing
in action, believed to be dead,
and my grief drizzles me awake to dawn . . .

The miracle of the mind prescient
please God no, only busy at its planting
and excavating Russian, German, English
selves electric and busy remapping
and presenting alternative histories.

So yes, now, finally
I've been given the perfect award for being human.
Poem, as always we salute you.

Ecstasies

The wing tip lifting
my body opening
lilacs entering your wide mouth.
They scent the entire water.
Storm. Storm clouds and rain slant on the windows.
How fast the parallel plane travels
small in our sky.
Whose toy?

You open wide
as I bend to check you out,
touch blood with my fingers.
Twilight office, empty
where I squat surrounding you,
embryo, celebrate with salt.

And I swear now, the bike
steadied as it flew out of his hands!

The fresh places you probed for gravel
so gentle as the gauze wiped grit
no panic, the young aunt steady
at my knee.

Alone on my pillows, clean after surgery.

The sun on our shoulders
adults whisper behind newspapers.
Surf bubbles we catch in pails. Heavy sand.
The salt tongue cups up from the wrist.

Between rails between ties our skate blades
hit perfectly, propel us on our way
to the rink. Horses steam on the ice.

Someone opens his eyes.

In the cold bar, I drink tea.

The door opens out
and in walks my brother.

On the phone, the lost
revive in your vocal cords
and you know nothing
more than the hour of arrival.

Sometimes as Einstein says time folds
an envelope in the pocket
and my robe opens
to fire on a rounding belly.

Where I am now,
every ecstasy dissolves
back into the pool,
the lap of waves,
the filled basin.

Acknowledgments

Thanks to the following magazines and books in which these poems appeared:

The Bread Loaf Anthology of Contemporary Nature Poetry. Ed. Robert Pack and Jay Parini. Hanover and London: University Press of New England: "Teaching, Hurt," "For Barbara, Who Brings Me a Green Stone in the Shape of a Triangle."

Cancer through the Eyes of Ten Women. Ed. Patricia Duncker and Vicky Wilson. London and San Francisco: Pandora, an imprint of HarperCollins: "Riverroad, Meandering Root," a sequence of twelve poems: "Repair," "Let's Consider the Consequences," "Weathering/Boundaries/What is Good," "Mu," "Breast/Fever," "Petting the Scar," "Fish–Belly–Mound," "For Barbara, Who Brings a Green Stone in the Shape of a Triangle," "Mapping/Bleating," "Bernini's Ribbon," "Nuts," "Who Does She Think She Is."

The Colorado Review: "Cobb's Hill Pond," "I Hear the Name of the Moon and Am Afraid," "Sarah among Animals," "Sarah's Response."

Judaism: "Isaac Stern's Performance," "Insomnia Again," "Vowels."

Laurel Review: Opening/Working/Walking.

Literature and Medicine: "Weathering/boundaries/what is good," "Riddle."

Nebraska English Journal: "Graffiti," "Bernini's Ribbon."

Ploughshares: "Breast/fever," "Service."

Southern Review: "Balance," "Petting the Scar," "From Your Mouth to God's Ear."

The Women's Review of Books: "Day-old Bargain," "Daylight Savings," "Chigger Socks," "For Barbara," "Trope," "Axe-earrings, abalone shell."

UNIVERSITY PRESS OF NEW ENGLAND

publishes books under its own imprint and is the publisher for Brandeis University Press, Dartmouth College, Middlebury College Press, University of New Hampshire, Tufts University, and Wesleyan University Press.

ABOUT THE AUTHOR

Hilda Raz is Associate Professor of English at the University of Nebraska, Lincoln, and is Editor-in-Chief of the award-winning literary quarterly Prairie Schooner. *Her previous books include* The Bone Dish *(1989)*, What is Good *(1988)*, *and* What Happens *(1986)*.

LIBRARY OF CONGRESS CATALOGING-IN-PUBLICATION DATA

Raz, Hilda.
   Divine honors / Hilda Raz.
       p. cm. — (Wesleyan Poetry)
   ISBN 0–8195–2248–1 (cloth : alk. paper) . — ISBN 0–8195–2249–X (pbk. : alk. paper)
    1. Breast—Cancer—Patients—Poetry. 2. Women patients—poetry.
I. Title. II. Series.
PS3568.A97D5   1997
811'.54—dc21   97–10481